Awakenings
THOUGHTS ON
Life

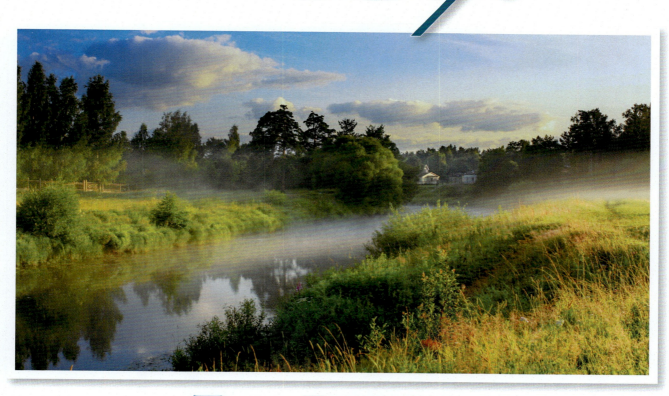

THE POETRY
of
JOHN HALL

ISBN: Softcover   978-1-5035-0947-4
        Hardcover   978-1-5035-0949-8
        EBook   978-1-5035-0948-1

Print information available on the last page

Rev. date: 09/07/2015

To order additional copies of this book, contact:
Xlibris
1-888-795-4274
www.Xlibris.com
Orders@Xlibris.com

And, special thanks to......

Special thanks to the Universe
for simply making me
for allowing me to speak and feel
allowing me to be

I see, I hear, I have a body
I exist right here, right now
and as I write these words for you
I simply wonder how

From cosmic dust we all were born
Miracle beyond our comprehension
From billions of years of experiments
the soup that created us, Universal intention

Yes, you can read this, I can write it
we can feel connected
But, if we try to understand
it cannot be dissected

So, special thanks to God himself
for allowing me to be
I'll do my best to share with you
the feelings that come through me....

John Hall

"South Park" is the name that we patients lovingly used to describe South Pacific Private Hospital where I undertook a 6 week drug and alcohol rehab programme. It was here that I began my journey, a journey to rediscover who I am.

This poem was the first poem that I recollect having ever written. Although I liked poetry at school, I had never really thought of writing. Whilst I was meditating one evening, it just came to me.

I did not write again until 2013. I was at the "Oneness" Retreat in the Hunter Valley which is hosted by Amir Zoghi. On the next page I share the poem that I wrote there.

"South Park"

Each day I prayed to God for peace, some help to ease my pain.
He heard me not, or so I thought, my prayers had been in vain.
I wish I'd listened harder then, for what he had to say
"My son, I love you, yes I do: Here's some light to guide your way."
It's off to South Pacific, John — the answers are all there.
"Look deep inside yourself," He said, "in answer to your prayer."

I arrived at South Pacific only five short weeks ago,
My life so full of dread and fear, of things I did not know.
To find the truth, begin the search, to pacify my fears
To find the lonely "Inner Child", I had not seen in years.

With lots of trepidation I settled in my bed,
To begin the fearful journey, which was only in my head.
To lectures Monday morning I went, with only thoughts of gain
I learned of co-dependence — the source of all my pain.

"Perhaps there's more to it than this?" I really had to know.
My life was such a misery, although it didn't show.
My job, my wife, my family: and all the toys I needed.
My life was really empty, I felt I had been cheated.
Inside I felt an emptiness that chilled me to the bone,
A deep, deep well of loneliness — I'd lived my life alone.

So off to group I trudged, with the crew from green
To investigate those issues which had lain so long unseen.
"As you tell your story, let your feelings flow.
Breath into them," Brad said, "just let those feelings go.
Tell where in your body that your anger lies
And I'll bring it to the surface before your very eyes."

Memories from my past, so long forbidden
Stirring deep in my soul, the pain long hidden.
To find the answers that God had sent
If only I had known what he had meant.

"Survivors" was a special week — 0 to 17 explored,
Those childhood feelings that had lain so long ignored.
Helen opened up my heart to those fears long unseen
So I could see how injured my little child had been.

My anger, my guilt, my pain, my shame
Are there to teach me, that is their aim.
Total love and joy is the natural state
To feel it, I need to remove my fear and hate.
The road less travelled is the one for me
The path to explore my spirituality.
With the 12 steps of AA to guide my way
To hear my higher power, every time I pray.

What did I learn during my five-week stay?
That I'm nearer to God each and every day.
That, to love myself, I need to love my brother.
That the purpose of our lives is to love one another.
That my feelings are the guideposts along the way
To total love and joy and the peace for which I pray.
That I am part of God and he is part of me
And if I listen to my feelings, He will set me free.

John H.
17 July 2000

3

The Retreat

I came with a touch of trepidation
To explore my heart and soul
To understand my essence
To make me complete and whole

I need to know my purpose
The reason that I am
To dig below the surface
and to be a better man

To see the One in each of us
To understand their pain
To thank them for the lessons
That allow my soul to gain

The lesson on the path of life
Is that there is only one
I am he, he is she and she is me
We really are all ONE

The sense of separation
Is a false belief, for sure
The question is, if this true
Then where to look for more?

Outside myself? Inside of you?
The answer isn't clear

It's hidden in the strangest place
Where you'd never think to peer

The answer isn't here or there
or hidden in a prayer
The answer to your every wish
is right inside of you

The question then
Is how to find
this hidden gem of peace?
The answer may surprise you 'cause
It's really simple so...

Just breathe in here
And breathe in now
And learn the how
of releasing from the torment
The answer is so simple - true
Stay in the present moment!

How can that be?
You may well ask
The answer is so clear...
The Universe itself is hidden
deep inside of you, my dear!

JH - 26 August 2013

Following the "Retreat" in August 2013, poetry just seemed to "flow" — I found myself writing almost every day.

The process of writing seems somehow cathartic — it seems to help me process what is going on in my mind!

On the pages that follow I share some of what I wrote over the following months. From time to time I will comment upon what was going on for me although, in most cases, the poetry can speak for itself. ...

"Awakenings"

Awakening of spirit
stirring in the soul
images, thoughts coalesce
making me feel whole

Feeling as one with life
leave behind my strife
pain is torn asunder
and just left behind

Quietening my mind
being present to
the feelings of my spirit, yes
feeling kind of blue

Leave behind my story
script of my past woe
being present to this moment
everywhere I go

Breathing into stillness
breathing into peace
feel the breeze upon my skin
feeling quite at ease

Listening to music
Peer Gynt, in fact
gentle tones caress my ears
leaving behind my lack

Feeling love in this sweet moment
nothing else to feel
love is all around me
only it is real

All else is illusion
story to leave behind
listen to my spirit
and ignore my mind

Mind is tool of ego
sent to me to distract
from what is real
my life has been an act

An actor in the story
is what I have been
ignoring the truth for far too long
ignoring the unseen

If I cannot see it
can it be for real?
Or is the spirit longing
for the love I feel

In this tender moment
all just seems OK
wrap this peace around me
as I go through my day

Can I be observer
Can I see what's real
Can I still my mind for long enough
to very, simply feel

Feel the truth that's all around me
everywhere I look
life is just a circus
just a storybook

As I ponder on this feeling
that all I see is false
Life is so deceiving
simply feel my pulse

As the blood is rushing
into my soul and heart
Can I use this moment
for another start?

In this present moment
is everything I need
nothing more required
nothing here to heed

Yes, this present moment
is all that I am given
to live my life
need not be so driven

Ignore the thoughts
that invade my mind

Simply feel into my soul
and leave my fears behind

In this present moment
as I simply breath
my tears are welling
my ego does recede

The joy of life is simply lived
in the here and now
learning to still my mind
is the why and how

The question I have often asked
is "Does my existence matter?"
do I just delude myself
listening to all that chatter?

Yes, methinks I do
delude myself for sure
I have this present moment
how could I want for more?

Poetry

Poetry, like music
is meant to stir the soul
At times it tears us apart
At times it makes us whole

When I put pen to paper
I very clearly see
The message is not something that
is coming here from me

When I am writing I do feel
connected to divine
The words just flow from somewhere else
They feel somehow sublime

I feel that I'm connected to
something more than mind
When I am writing poetry
I leave ego behind

The words are channelled through me
I know that to be true
Somehow I am connected
that part of me reflected
In you

Yes, when I read a poem
I feel the love in words
describing others feelings
and life seems less absurd

The words do flow from Universe
from energy it seems
We do not feel it often but
it comes to us in dreams

Sometimes it comes with music
and sometimes comes in prayer
That feeling of connection when
I know there's more out there

I am more than body
I have to have a soul
how else could I be connected to
be greater than the whole?

The words they just come to me
I do not think of them
Somehow they flow on through me
and down into my pen

The pen just glides along and says
what needs to be said right now
The truth of just this moment
I do not know the how

I know the words are from my heart
the essence of my being
They are not from mind it seems
The process is so freeing

Yes, I write my poetry
for no one else but me
But sometimes when I'm sharing
Others then can see

The beauty all around them
The beauty that's within
That they are whole, complete
There is no such thing as sin

Everything is perfect
As it is right now
And so are they, eternally
There is no why, no how

So, poetry just keeps me present
Whether writing or reading
Music does the same sometimes
The truth is not misleading

There truth is there inside of us
The secret is to find
A way to connect to self
Connect with the divine

"The Music Of My Life"

What is this music that I hear when I still my mind?
How is it that it helps me to leave my fear behind?
It's sweet caress just washes over me and leaves me feeling warm
It somehow eases the pain inside and makes me less forlorn

The music of the Universe is there for us to hear
all we need to do is listen and it does become quite clear
It's more the sound of silence than music in the literal sense
but somehow when we hear it, it makes such a difference

It seems the sounds of Universe are flowing all around
and when we can tune in to them, that softly flowing sound
we somehow connect with self, and Universe as well
and we seem to know that truth is in the rising swell

The energy of Universe, it flows through each of us
and if we listen to it then we give up all the fuss
The fuss of life we leave behind when we can hear and feel
the music of the Universe, it truly makes us heal

As one with God and everything, it simply makes us whole
it does not speak to us through ears, it speaks to our sweet soul
It is in everything we see, and everything we do
and, yes, you may be surprised to hear, it even is in you

This music is the energy of life, it's simple ebb and flow
and, yes, it is there with us, everywhere we go
But, oftentimes we are too busy, too tied up in things
involved too much in busyness to hear the magic that it brings

This music is the breath of life, the very breath of soul
it moves our inner spirit and it allows us to be whole
it allows us to connect to self and every living thing
and when we allow it to flow we simply want to sing

We want sing aloud in joy for all that we are seeing
for simply being here today, for very simply, being
Oh, yes, this music rocks the Universe, it is just everywhere
in every single thing we see, we need to be aware

So, pause a while, just take a breath, connect unto your core
and let this music flow through you, just feel it's gentle score
Oh, yes, the hand of God directs, this music of the soul
and when you simply let it flow your life will seem quite whole

"You're Amazing!"

Has anyone told you of late
that you are just amazing
The light of you just simply shines
The light of you is blazing

You blaze with light
from things unseen
A child of God, no less
and everything about you sings
of his amazing grace

He made you simply perfect
Reflection of divine
Please just understand then
when I say that you do simply shine!

If you can just pause then for a while
and contemplate what's real
you will see as clear as day
you are more than what you feel

The magic of reality
inspired from the start
To see the beauty shines within
from your just perfect heart

When God (The Universe) created you
unique
He threw away the blueprint 'cause
he knew it was perfect

He knew he could not better what
he had done with you
So, he then created someone else
equally different and true

Perfection is the truth of us
of each and everyone
Perfection in the making
Reflection of the "One"

Reflection, then, of God we are
Reflection of what's real
Perfection then in everyone
It almost seems unreal

So, when I look upon your face
and look into your soul
I see the glory of it all
Each of us is made whole

We all have inside of us
what it takes to be
reflection of the Universe
The perfection that is me!

The Mask

It is another Monday then
I have to face the world again!
To toil my life away
And for what, I cannot say

The weekend's gone
and so is peace
The peace of being me
I will put on my Batman suit
and pretend I'm someone else
When all I want to be
Is Myself

I look at others
And I often ask
Who are they behind the mask
Or is it just me?

What do they know that I don't know?
Is there something I can't see?
How do they seem so happy when
I struggle to love my life
And who I am

What is it like to love yourself?
I often ask as I look at them
Am I God's failure, his mistake
Can I not love myself?
What is his take?
Can I not love my life?

I seem to feel empty inside
I want to go away and hide
In alcohol, drugs and busyness
The busyness that numbs my mind
To where there's peace
So I can find
Some silence from
The endless, mindless chatter
To where I feel that I can matter

Why did God make me so?
I really wish that I could know
Am I his child and does he care
What I think and feel
And why I am here

Please God, just give me joy
Like I had when a little boy
So full of joy and innocence
When I thought I knew
What my life meant

So, can I go into the world
With love and joy
Life unfurled
In all it's magic
For me to see
Who I am, the real me?

Gaia – Mother Earth

The planet that we live upon
Is under stress you know
The pollution we have created
Gives us nowhere else to go

The truth of this is so, so sad
Destroy our home, we must be mad
The question then is simply said
What can we do about it?

To create a better world
One that's free from all this pain
The pain of destroying everything
In our search for earthly gain

The answer then, perhaps,
Is to love our mother, Earth
So that we leave a planet
That is not so dearth
Of resources, so very slim
That our children can't survive
To leave a planet that can revive

So please just be conscious
And live your life complete
Without the toys
And other stuff
That never seems to be enough

So be "aware" of what you do
And understand this truth
That we are one with everything
Including Mother Earth

A simple life can bring real joy
It's simple, precious moments
That mean the most to all of us
And will relieve this torment

Prayer, God and the Universe

I pray to God most every day
And ask for help along the way
The way of life we truly need
A healthy, wealthy life
A life of joy without the fears
Of something going wrong
A life of joy and happiness
A life without the tears

He answers me in funny ways
To keep me on the road
The road to what is joy and love
A life without the load
He tells me don't look back
Don't look ahead he also says
The only place to be is here
We "create" from here and now

Right now will set you free, he says
Stay in the present moment
Stay focused on the "here" and "now"
To silence the opponent
The enemy is not "here" and "now"
It cannot be in the present

The enemy is when we lose ourselves
To the past or the future
When we are there
and not right "here"
We lose our sense of presence

We disconnect from our true selves
and cannot use our power
The power to "create" from love
The things that make our future
Which, when arrives,
becomes another present moment!

The present moment is all we have
From here we create the how
The how of how our life is lived
Takes place from here right now
The future will unfold for me
The way is should, somehow

When I think about the future
And am not right here and now
The power to create is gone
And he can't talk to me

It's only when I'm present that
He helps me feel and see
What is the truth
What can be done
With some real clarity

The truth be known
That life is lived
From where I am right now
It will unfold just as it should
Without my help, somehow

14

When I am here and just present to
The possibility
It really comes together then
Without input from me
The future is so simply put
It is a series of present moments
One after the other, so simple said
But challenging to live....

It can be hard to stay right here
When pressure to abscond exists
And be in past or future
Is bearing down upon us from
Everything around us
When we are planning, doing,
And simply not "being"
We need the present to ground us!

So that we are truly seeing
The truth of this bold statement
That God is right here with us right now
And only here and now And from this "now"
Is where we create our future
Not in our plans,
Nor in our hopes
Not in our sense of future
Our power is is the present

I'd we could only see this clearly
And truly understand it
We are creators of our lives
From here right in this moment!

It sounds like I am harping then
Upon this word the present
But truly understand this when
You are in prayer
That God can only hear you then
From this so precious moment.

The energy of God, the Universe
Is here in all around us
It is in every single thing
Not out there somewhere outside us
So, go inside to what is real
The truth is just astounding
That you are God
This really is quite grounding

So when you are with present, now
You are as one with God
And from this place it truly seems
We really can create our dreams
Yes, we can, I truly know
And hope that you can too
Be present then
And from this place
Dreaming will come true

Morning...

'tis another day, I fear
Where my future will unfold
The story of my life today
Is going to be told.

How will it look, I ask myself?
Another day of task
It this what is to come of it
Just looking at my mask?

Or can I see behind it all
To feel the truth of me?
That I am here to feel and do
Not only what I see?

What do I see behind the fear?
The fear of being there?
When in reality the truth
Is that I should just be here?

Here, what does it really mean?
It means to be at peace
With who I am
And savour the present moment
Present to each moment then
Rather than in the past
A victim of my fears
The fears I have created
by not being here and now..

The past is gone and won't be back
The future is the same
The only place to be, I'm told
Is in the present moment.

The question then is
How to stay right here?
When the future screams for me to do
Something to overcome my fear
When, my goals should be, I know
To be right here, to be right now!
To "breathe" into the moment
To listen to my soul
And stay as one
with this present moment!

I know today will be
A canvas for me to paint
What will unfold
I ask myself...
What will my actions hold?
Reality, then, is to be just here..
To just be "present"
What does that mean?
To think, to feel?
I can't be sure
But what I know for sure
Is that my life means more..
More than my past...
More than my thoughts...
My existence has to matter
Life is surely more than this
The constant, mindless chatter.

Be still my thoughts
Be still my heart
Be "still" and feel the present
The "stillness" here
The "stillness" now
Is peace and reminiscent
Of when I listen to my soul
I And feel as one with life
As one with all
As one with God
As One with you
And one with every soul
It is the only time I feel
That my life is whole

The answer to my dilemma then
Is to be as one with breath
To feel each breath as if it is
The only moment I that I exist.
Which is just true
And has to be
The only goal I have
To listen to each breath
And stay just here
In this present moment!

My goal today then
Is just a simple one
To breath as if my last
It may well be
Who is to know?
Let me just be present!

Present to life
Present to now
Present to each true feeling
Not in the future
Nor in the past
Just how?
Just here, right now?

Only Love Is Real

"Is love for real" I sometimes ask
And others ask more often
How is it then that simple truth
Is so easily forgotten?

Only love is real
All else is false
Love is our natural state
But ego comes along our way
And distracts us with it's take

It's take on life is that we need
The things that we collect
But truth be known, it's nothing more
Than our sad intellect

Our mind is not reality
It's more an ego-driven script
That keeps us poor and starving
Collecting more exciting things
In search of love, it really is
But does not know the truth
Our complex mind has lost it's way
In searching for the truth
The truth of us, that we exist
And that is all there is!

We search for love in others too
When really what we crave
Is love, just love - the love of self
Admit it's true, admit it yes
That all I really have is here
And all I have is now
And that the truth of it is this..
Here and now is where real love exists

It is inside of me, I know
When I am in the flow
When I am just connected
To the energy I know
The flow of life is all there is
And it is here and now
The past is a reflection of
When I had lost my way
The only truth is that love exists
Right here, right now, today

This moment is a treasure then
That I can only feel
When I am present
To the truth
That only love is real!

Prayer

"Please bless me Lord" I hear you pray
As you pass along this path today
Please let me stay in your Holy grace
That I may serve the human race

I know you sent your only son
To show the way our lives should run
He showed us miracles could be performed
By all of us when thinking is reformed

To live like this we must be reborn
To help the poor and those forlorn
To live in love of our fellow man
We must listen to him for our master plan

"What's his plan for me?" I hear you say
'tis to find your peace in him today
To live with hope and without the fear
That you seem to have almost every year

Live in Love and live without those fears
That you have had for all these years
That would be so cool, if it were true
That I live like this, that I live like you

Reflections

Is my life a reflection
Of the things I've said and done?
Or is it more an action
Of the wishes of the ONE?

I wish I knew the answer
To the question I've just asked.
Or is more an illusion
Just hidden behind the mask?

The mask of life's illusion
That says it's all for real.
The physical delusion
That life is what I feel?

Is what I feel reality?
I ask myself each day.
I know for sure it isn't true
But it seems to hold it's sway.

The mask of my reality
Is what I seem to see
But in the stark, cold light of day
I know it isn't me.

So, what is true?
And what is real?
The answer seem so clear
That what I feel, if not this fear
Is love, I think, my dear.

So can this mean
I am not sure
That life is more than fear?
Can it mean, perhaps, perchance
That love can reign so clear?

I do not know, I only hope
That this is true, maybe?
That Love is all there is to it
In my reality?

What does this mean?
I am not sure
But maybe if it's true
Then you are me?
And we are one?
And I am part of you?

Let's just assume that this is fact
And fear is just surreal
Then love is true
And fear is false
And love is mine to feel.

To love is where the truth is at
And how is this you ask?
Just be in the present moment
And fear is just a mask
When in the present moment
You only can feel the love
The overwhelming abundance
That comes from the above
The one in every moment
Is the feeling that you seek
It's there for every of us
The humble and the meek
The strong, the ever silent
The stoic and proud
It matters not where you come from
The love, it will abound!

Stay in the present moment
If it is the peace you seek
The moment now is all we have
The past, however bleak
'Tis in the present moment
That the answer lies, for sure
To all your trepidations
To ensure your life is more.

'Tis in the present moment
That the future is in store
From this creative presence
We create our thoughts, and more
From here and now
No matter what
We think may be ahead
This is simply a reflection
Of what we thought and said.

So say it loud and say it clear
Tomorrow is all mine
I will create my future then
When my feelings do align
With what I feel and what I do
And what I know is true
I simply trust to be myself
In what I say and do

The reflection here is so much more
Than what I simply think
It's more about my feelings then
Than what my mind creates
My thinking is illusion
And my feelings are for real
They are a real reflection
Of the Only ONE ideal!

"Nothing Matters"

As I looked both inside and outside myself
for the meaning of my life
I've come to realise there is more
than just my fear and strife

The pain I feel most all the time
I've come to understand
is when I disconnect from self
let go of my maker's hand

I've looked in drugs and alcohol
I've looked in love as well
but what I've come to understand
is that this life is simply hell
if I don't learn to love myself
and connect to my sweet soul

As I searched for meaning
I followed a winding road
to find the truth inside myself
to ease my heavy load

The truth is nothing matters
other than to be right here
In this present moment
there simply is no fear

When I think I want some thing or other
to make me feel alive
I now know it is ego
telling me it's lies

Nothing can make me happy
other than truth of self
This simple present moment
is my only wealth

So, chase not things or people
to make yourself complete
Be at peace with who I am
and life will be replete

Replete with gorgeous moments
where everything's OK
The only thing that I really need
is to savor this sweet day

This day of present moments
be present to the love
that exists inside of my sweet soul
connected to God above

Yes, I'm all that matters
to Universe, I'm sure
stay in touch with present
and long for nothing more

The Pen Is Mightier Than The Sword

When I write my feelings down
they somehow seem to be
the truth at that sweet moment
the truth that sets me free

If I just keep my feelings there
roaming inside my head
Ego does take over and
I somehow get misled

It takes me to conclusions that
make me think it's wrong
But when I write them downs it seems
they do not feel so strong

It is somehow cathartic
to capture them with pen
They seem to leave me all alone
and I can go on then

When I write down what's going on
deep inside my head
I feel somehow relieved from them
and feel not so much dread

When I read the words of others
captured with a pen
I feel just so uplifted and
above the realm of men

Words on paper lift men up
to things above themselves
But sword just tears men down
to think of no one else

The words of men just captured
by the mighty pen
allow us all to connect to
past and future when

All is good and all is kind
and we can feel uplifted
by their simple words of joy
it isn't even scripted

The proof lies in the numbers
of books that people read
Of poets great from yesteryear
Rumi, oh, so gifted!

Of Kahlil Gibran and Shakespeare too
of all have gone before me
of all the wonderful things they wrote
to simply make me free

Yes, pen can uplift my day
and as I simply read them
I know for sure that I can feel
what it is they say

When I put pen to paper
to express just how I feel
The simple act of writing proves
that my thoughts are not real

They seem real enough to me
at the time of writing
But when I read them later
they seems so less inviting

23

Other than to remind me of
the feelings at that time
when I was feeling sad or blue
somehow seeking rhyme

Seeking rhyme and rhythm
Seeking to know myself
Attempting impossible
To simply know the self

But put your thoughts on paper
and you will simply see
the purpose of your writing is
to very, simply be

To be as one with Universe
to simply understand
the truth of life, it's mystery
I sit with pen in hand

To capture what I'm feeling
To say what comes to mind
To understand the truth of me
to leave my fears behind

Oh, yes, just give me pen to write
and I can change the world
I'll touch a soul or two
or even change the world!

Because, you see, it is quite clear
that thoughts have changed the world
The eloquence of poetry
expresses why we're here

We're here to "feel"
the good and bad
So we can simply see
that all we simply have to do
is very, simply "be"

In "being" we can see the truth
of who we really are
and it is in the books we read
that we can see afar

Afar from where we are today
Afar from pain and fear
and understand the joy
of simply being here!

"Sweet Embrace"

Dearest Lover
I write this for you
so you will know
what's going on

Going on
inside of me
in this simple heart of mine
my wish for you
I implore you
follow heart
it is sublime

I caress you
do undress you
in my mind

Stroke your hair
oh, so, golden
sweet temptation
Oh, so fair

Stroke your neck
press into you
feel your body
next to mine

Hold you to me
love runs through me
and you feel it
in your soul

I just want to
simply hold you
wash away
your every care

Can I hold you
and then I fold you
into me
where all is safe

Forget tomorrow
just be right here
let me tease you
let me please you
just by simply holding you

Can we do it
just get through it
may I rub your back
Oh, just so gently
massage away your fear

I look at you
then I see it
that so salty tear
I will hold you
swaying gently
melt into each other
gently swaying
to the music
of our souls

Sweet caresses
Heaven blesses
simply leave behind
our fears

25

Star crossed lovers
holding tightly
hoping night will last forever
but the dawn will come, we know

So, just be here
gently swaying
also praying
that we can stay
like this, forever
No we can't dear
you and I know
life goes on

So we must part
I feel your heart
knowing that it is just too short
But, in meantime
may I hold you
even if for just a while

Show me your face
in this embrace
let me stroke your
gentle brow

Yes, I feel it
your chest heaving
as I melt into you
whole

Can we embrace
if just for a moment
escape our torment
for a while

Please just show me
how you're feeling
please just give me
a gentle smile

Don't ignore it
what you're feeling
give into it
for a while

We can stand here
stand together
gently hugging
into time

If I could I would just hold you
feel you melt into my soul
two together, as if forever
feeling as if we were whole

"A Letter From God"

Here is a letter I received
Just the other day
Written to me by the Universe
to help me on my way

Dearest John, want you to know
that I am on your side
There is nothing you need fear
nothing from which to hide

You were made by me to feel
the joys that life can bring
Made from formless energy
You were made to dance and sing

All the things that you think of
that make you want to run
are simply thoughts, unreal
You are my favourite son

Yes, breath into truth
and know who you really are
Energy of life complete
made from a former star

From cosmic dust did I create
All you see around
Every single living thing
to live in peace and harmony
in happiness abound

You were made to live in joy
to know you are complete
I gave you everything you need
to live your life, replete

Replete with everything you need
to live your life in love
of who you really are, image of the divine
made to live in harmony so you can really shine

Yes, you were made complete
with everything you need
to live a life of joyousness
in everything succeed

So go ahead each and every day
with this thought in mind
that everything is perfect, as is
and leave your fear behind

Life is perfect and so are you
and so is everyone
Reflection of the Universe
made from stars and ancient sun

When your fears do overwhelm
just breath into this moment
and from that place you truly can
just leave behind the torment

The torment that your mind makes up
It simply is not real
Just breath into this present time
and focus on what you feel

Because the only thing that exists
is in the here and now
Every other thing you think
is a game that's played by ego, yes
Bringing you undone, somehow

27

I See YOU...

When I look into your eyes
what is it at I see?
I see your soul inside of you
as you were meant to be

I see more than your story, yes
Not your body nor your face
I see perfection as it is
your simply amazing grace

I see past your story and
I see just so much more
I see the little boy or girl
who need not ask for more

I see your grace, I sense your space
I feel I understand
the meaning of your life
the reason you're so grand

If you could just be at peace with this
the perfection that you are
Understanding how you came to be
from home you are not far

At home with what is here today
at home with your sweet soul
You would not ask for anything more
you'd know that you are whole

Reflection of the Universe
Made perfect by God's hand
You wouldn't look outside yourself
to simply understand

That who you are matters to all of us
you were sent here to connect
to all of us so that we could learn
about ourselves, when we simply connect

Connecting to the truth of life
to who we really are and what is real
We need not look to others
to somehow feel worthwhile
inside ourselves we can feel our soul

"Crossing The Line"

Will I ever cross the line
to what I can become
rather than just sit back here
and to my fears succumb?

The line is there, I see it clear
to what I want, what I can be
So, why do I feel such fear?
When all I want to do, is simply just be me

I want to be the me I was born to be
not the me I have become
I want to be the me, set free
a part of Universe, the "One"

I want to be a me of who I can be proud
so that I can raise my voice and say it out loud
A me who does what needs be done
not doing the bidding of everyone

A me who honours what is real
not victim of the fears I feel
A me not regretting my past
of things not done, of things I've passed

Of things that I could have done
that I did want to do
but I was simply too afraid
comparing myself to you

Compared myself to everyone
thought that they were all just better
Not true of course, but at the time,
I was so insecure in who I was,
what I could do, my fears did simply fetter

They fettered me like concrete to the me
I thought I was but, truth be known,
was all a sham of gigantic proportions
Ego imposed, my fears were real,
too enormous to surmount
Unable to just cross the line,
image was paramount

So, if I was to cross the line, what would it take?
Could I take the step, the step across the line,
where there is no turning back
not going back to what I think
I am across the line I simply fear
that I'm not up to what I think I can

That white line, of which I'm afraid to cross
what is it then that I do fear,
afraid of some kind of a loss
I know exactly what it is I fear,
afraid to articulate
because other folk may hear
and judge me,
of that I'm really afraid

I'm not afraid that I'm too weak
or that I cannot do it
of what I am afraid is that I can do it
and then there is no turning back
I'll have to leave my crutches behind
and give myself no slack
To do the things I've done
of which I am so fond

My addictions I will leave behind,
my God I can't imagine
what life is like without them,
the thought of it does sadden

Ego

Some say the ego is our enemy
It distracts us with the chatter
That fills our minds and takes us away
From things that really matter

I'm not so sure that this is true
Ego must serve a purpose
For the power, God, who created us
Would not make life a circus!

So please help me understand
Why Ego does exist
The endless, mindless chatter then
Why does it persist?

In telling me that I'm not good enough
Without the things and other stuff
That I collect along the way
And that I need to change myself
When all along I should understand
That I was made by the maker's hand

That God exists inside of me
And inside everyone
And everything is just alright, somehow
As it is, right here and now!

"Grief"

I grieve for me, the me I could have been
I grieve for me, the me I have not seen
of things unsaid, of things undone
of things I left unsaid and songs I left unsung

I grieve for who I am, for who I have become
for not just being here, recognising that I am one
One with everything, just part of this sweet life
I grieve because I know the truth, there is no fear or strife

I grieve because I've learned there is no going back
I grieve because I felt such loneliness, such emptiness and lack
I could have had a life so full of play and joy
I should have listened to my heart when I was just a boy

Should have taken the path that I was called to follow
and I would not be sitting here feeling just so hollow
knowing that I've wasted time, frittered away my past
doing things to impress others, not following my heart

Yes, I grieve today, because I feel such pain
chasing earthly pleasures that simply bring no gain
when I could have lived as if each breath were my last
seizing every moment then, not living in the past

My grief is overwhelming me, engulfing me in tears
washing over me, filling me with fears
I'm feeling so alone, so sad I want to cry
looking back on my life, the way it's passed me by

My grief is telling me that I need to change
focus on the present now, let go of my rage
Let go of the past right now, live my life right here
Live my life as if there is nothing left to fear

Focus on the joy I have, the simple joy of being
breath into this sweet moment, here, it is so much more freeing
Grieve not for things I cannot change, grieve not for yesterday
grieve not for friends I've lost, let fear not hold it's sway

Let the sunshine wash my grief away, as it does the dark
Let the present moment cleanse me now, ignite my holy spark
Let the joy of simply being here fill my heart with love
connected to every living thing, connected to above

"It's 5 a.m."

It's 5.00 a.m., I sit and ponder
cigarette in hand
In the east the sun is rising
waking up the land

Birds are singing
I am clinging
to remnants of my dreams
Is life what it seems?

Earth is warming
birds are swarming
welcoming the day
Inside I'm crying
sick of trying
to live another way

Breeze is blowing
gently showing
I have another chance

To change my thinking
stop my sinking
into the abyss

Abyss of depression
what's the lesson
I should learn today?

Stay just present
to the moment
fear will dissipate

Can I do this
get right through this
love myself today

Yes, I can do it
thinking as I here sit
there is another way

Change my focus
change my process
Simply enjoy my day

Mother Nature does remind me
if I just be present
very simply be
here in her presence
simply being free

Free to ponder
gaze in wonder
on another day

JH 25 November 2014

"Meaning"

"What is the meaning of my life?"
I very often ask
"What is there to see
if I look behind the mask?"

Behind the mask
that I so often see
the mask of who I am
and who I think is me

Behind duality
behind the ego's curse
behind the things I think are me
behind the earthen hearse

Behind the body and the mind
the things I think are real
when, truth be truly understood
I am just what I feel

I am emotion, energy
in fact I'm nothing more
than pure energy
of that I feel so sure

Energy is all I am
the energy of life
and all the petty things
the struggles and the strife
are not the truth of who I am
they are just ego's calls
to listen to what is not real
the juggling of the balls

The juggling of the endless chatter
going on inside
the struggle just to understand
from what it is I hide

I struggle just to understand
what I am supposed to do
so that I can survive
and get along with you

I pretend to be someone
other than who I really am
in an effort to get along
and, somehow, escape this sham

This sham that I am simply
my body and my mind
when, truth be known, it seems to me
I'd prefer to leave this play behind

This game that I play
as I pretend to be
someone other than
the truth of who is me

If I am honest to myself
and simply calm my mind
I know the truth of who I am
much more than just this man

Much more than just a simple man
much more than what I think
Complexity in who I am
it just leads me to drink

In drink I seem to quell the storm
the questions that I ask
so what is going on
the truth behind the mask?

So, "Who am I?"
"Why am I here?"
These questions seek an answer
and when I ponder upon these issues
I seem just a romancer

Romancer, yes, not practical
can I function in this life?
Behind anxiety and fear
escaping all the strife?

Maybe I can come up with what is real
behind the endless questioning
am I just what I feel?

Maybe yes and maybe no
the answer seems elusive
Behind the endless questioning
can I just be effusive?

Effusive about what seems real
when I just ask the question
the answer seems so simple, yes
It's hardly worth a mention

The answer is that I am real
not in my mind it seems
and when I seek to feel
the answer lies in dreams

In dreams I do escape
the grind I face each day
and, in this place,
my fears do not hold their sway

Can it be that in my dreams
I truly understand
what my life is all about
my life I can understand

To understand the truth, behind the great illusion
the truth of who I really am, behind this great
delusion
Behind the chatter, behind the noise lies truth that I
can see
the truth, if simply known, that I was meant to be

JH 20 Feb 2015

"Longing"

As I look upon the moon
beaming down through the cloud
I gaze upon the starlight, blue
I reminisce out loud

I reminisce of days gone by
perhaps they were better times
a longing for a better life
Oh, how the years just fly!

A longing ache just fills my heart
I feel so all alone
My wistful look betrays the truth
I know not who I am

I long to truly understand
the reason I am here
my life is such a mystery
I cannot bear the fear

The fear that I'm not good enough
the thought I don't belong
the endless searching through the years
disconnected from the throng

The throng of all humanity
from which I feel apart
I long to feel connection to
the feelings of the heart

At times I've felt OK it seems
when I was there with you
but when I see you in my dreams
I feel just somehow blue

The wistful cloud through which the moon does peer
seems to me to cry
and as I gaze upon the night
the minutes drag on by

I long again to feel your love
connection to the truth
of who I am and why I'm here
the enthusiasm of my youth

As I gaze upon the moonlight, calm
the haunting does return
the memories of yesterday
the things for which I yearn

"Sleep"

I go to sleep again tonight
looking for some brief respite
from all the troubles of my day
In sleep they all just fade away

Into that bliss of night time slumber
I drift away, my fears of endless number
seem so small that I forget
the pain I feel, sleep full of regret

I drift into my dreams, with pleasure
In that space I do not remember
how small I feel during the day
my fears and troubles just fade away

Oh, I love my night time so
where, in that space, I somehow know
that all is good and I'm OK
prepare to face another day

In my dreams I somehow feel
that what I dream is somehow real
My days are dreams
and my dreams are true
during the night I am not so blue

My dreams take on a life of their own
I overcome the fears that I have known
I dream of things unseen, unsaid
I overcome all my fears and dread

Can my dreams tell me who I am?
That I am much more than this fearful man?
Am I up to this game of life I fear so much?
Is there hope for me, overcome my stuff?

The stuff that causes me to stumble?
Am I just a man, evermore so humble?
Can I awaken to a feeling of bliss and joy?
That feeling I had when just a little boy?

That feeling I had when I was so young?
that feeling before I became high strung?
That joy of greeting another day?
When all I knew was that I'd be OK?

Yes, give me sleep, just give me some peace
In my quiet slumber, my fears do cease
I dream of a better place to be
I dream of what it's like to just be free

Free of worry, free of fear?
Free of anxiety, where my future's clear?
Free to be what I was meant to be
Free to simply revel in being me?

Yes, when I arise to face my day
am I able to keep my fears at bay?
Focus on this moment of quiet peace
In this moment my fears do cease

So, here I am to face another day
Can I live it differently, in another way?
Can I stay just here, in this present tense
where why I'm here can make more sense?

Can I live as one with what I have got?
Understanding that I have the lot?
Everything that I need to thrive
Simply enjoy the feeling that I am alive?

When I'm awake I hear endless chatter
my mind deceives, telling me what I think does matter
but I know that what it says just isn't true
ego needs to tell me what to do

But I know way deep down inside
that there is no need to fear, no need to hide
Listen to my heart, it will lead me home
to where all is good, no need to roam

No need to roam in search of this and that
the present moment is where it is at
This present moment, my soul to keep
just like the joy I find in sleep

JH 6 November 2014

"Thankfulness"

I am thankful for my body
it houses my soul
Thankful for my spirit
makes me feel quite whole

I am thankful
for another day
As I breath into it
and start along the way

I feel sweet music
each step along the way
Staying with what's present
keeps my fears at bay

Fears appear when I'm not present
or dwelling on the past
yet I know that if I'm thankful
the pain or fear won't last

In this present moment
thankful that I exist
in the simple here and now
The longings won't persist

Yes, I am so thankful
for each breath I take
and in the joy of being "here"
there can be no mistake

Thankful for family, thankful for my friends
Thankful for my daily chores
in this present moment,
here miracles portend

The miracle of existence
The miracle of life
Surely in this present place
I have no fear or strife

Take a step into it
into this present breath
Life is such a miracle
I think not now of death

Yes, thankfulness overwhelms me
as I start my day
and with each breath I feel gratitude
for each step along the way

JH 11 Feb 2015

"The Gift"

This gift I give myself, attending this retreat
It's something I can use with everyone I meet
The gift of finding out who I really am
knowing I can do far more than I thought I can

The truth that I now know, that I know for sure
is that I am worthy and deserve so much more
Looking in the mirror now I can truly see
who I truly am and what I was meant to be

I look into my eyes and now I see my soul
I've come to understand that I am truly whole
Now, I feel at peace and leave story behind
live my life right now, to myself be kind

Learnt that I will only accept the love I think I'm
worth
I know this has been the case ever since my birth
If I can love myself I can set my spirit free
Truly learn to love myself, simply being me

I now know I'm beautiful, made in Universal love
knowing now my body's made to fit me like a glove
Knowing that the little me, the one I sometimes be
can play a bigger game, knows how to be free

Oh, yes, the bigger me, I now see in the mirror
Oh, yes, the perfect me reflects back even clearer
Yes, I give the gift of love unto myself
and, now I'm capable of giving it to someone else

Love is "unconditional" - no expectations in return
I came to the retreat for this lesson to learn
I can apply it to myself and to others too
and play a bigger game and to myself be true

Yes, the "One " Retreat has taught me this and more
All I need to do is tune on in and listen to it's score
I need only look inside and listen to my heart
and I can simply watch, as my fears depart

JH 12 October 2014

"Why?"

Why do I do what I do each day?
What is it that drives me to live my life this way?
Is it my ego that tells me what to do?
Or, am I doing what I know for me is true?

Good questions that I ask
as I sit here with my pen
What is there behind the mask
that tells me how and when?

Do I love each thing I do
or is it all just habit?
Do I control my destiny
Or am I just a rabbit?

Hopping from task to task
just to keep myself so busy
that I don't have to deal with thought
from whence all my pain is brought

My thoughts run round and round inside
this empty head of mine
In busyness I seek to hide
avoiding life, sublime

So, why do I do the things I do
that make my life so empty?
when I could do the things that count
and live a life of plenty?

Sometimes I do the things I love
and in that space I feel
the truth of who I really am
and I know that place is real

In that place of love I find
the truth behind my mask
that I am one with universal mind
and I'm up to every task

If I can sit in peace right here
being present to what I'm doing
I can feel my heart and soul
a place that's quite renewing

If I just did the things I love
or learn to love what must be done
I'd spend my day in peace and love
as part of what is "One"

Of course the truth is eluding me
when I am just too busy
doing things from habit or need
rather than just simply "being"

Yes, if I can just be present to
whatever is going on
even when I feel my fear
breath into it, accepting

Accepting what it is I feel
not avoiding it by "doing"
Even fear can be my friend, I suspect
it tells me what I'm avoiding

I'm avoiding the truth of now
of each and every breath
which is all I really have
until I face my death

I'm not afraid of death at all
and sometimes I look forward to it
because in death I would not have to deal
with the fears I face, if I could just get through it

It's really life I fear, not death
I'm afraid my life is worthless
because I haven't done what I could
I've lived life on the surface

Rather than look underneath
the activities of my day
Appreciate the truth of my life
not let my fear hold sway

So, what can I do today
to live a life more freeing?
If I can just be present to
my present state of being

Just "being" in this moment, Yes!
Just ask myself what's real
Just ask myself what's going on?
What is it that I feel?

Breath into each experience
including all my fears
just sit with them a while to understand
the thoughts behind the tears

My thoughts are leading me astray
from the truth of who I'm being
Ego's little game
believing what I'm seeing

But what I see is not the truth
No, not the truth at all
I'm looking at the outward self
rather than the sun behind each squall

Behind each cloud lies a rainbow too
Behind my fear is love
Just need to look inside to feel
connection to above

Connection to the truth of life
The simple truth of "being"
in this present moment, yes
lies the love that I've been fleeing

JH 10 November 2014

"The Gift"

What if everything that happens to me
truly is a gift?
Could I use this moment
to my soul uplift?

If this pain that I am feeling
came to do me good?
Is it happening to me
to teach me what I should?

Could this anxious moment
be used to make me strong?
Could I use this lesson?
Learn to get along?

Could I gives thanks for it?
This pain that I do feel
Is it just reflection
of what is truly real?

Can I use this moment
make myself feel good?
Teaching me what I need to
do simply what I should?

Yes, I can know this
everything's OK
And from this sweet moment
set out on my way

On my way to a life
that is getting better
Writing the script of my life
follow to the letter

The gift I have been given
In this single thought
will just make me stronger
not be here for nought

Yes, what if....
every thought of my life
were for me to feel?
Understand it's meaning
no thought is that real

Thought is just a message
leading me along
the path to understanding
making myself strong

Yes, I can live this moment
focus on the fear
or I could change my state
appreciate I'm here

Thankful that I have a life
grateful for it all
Doing what must be done
so that I can walk tall

Gratitude overwhelms me
as I think on this
Now I understand it
what I have to do
Just step forward
to myself be true

Life will never be the same again
now I know the truth
I can face fears that
I have had since youth

Yes, behind the fear then
I can feel the strength
that I have inside me
bring it to the fore

Breathe into my centre
breath into my core
Yes, I know it now
Yes, I can be much more

Thank you Tony Robbins
for helping me to understand
that I can do much more
be a better man

[this poem came to me after watching a short Tony Robbins clip on YouTube called "What if....."]
JH 30 October 2014